"*Not a Hero* hums with life at the same time it steals your breath. A one-eyed man working up the courage to talk to a waitress, a one-armed butcher in the French countryside, an artist who stalks prey and paints masterpieces with blood, and young brothers careening down a hill in a wagon with clean laundry exploding on the sidewalk are all characters you become in these poems. And whether you survive the endless cold of the WWII trenches, or escape a slap from an alcoholic mother, or wait a year for your next MRI to have clear margins, or sweep into an autumn romance, you will be able to tell the story as if you were there. Christiansen will stall your heart with his honesty and reward you with his craft: ghazal, haibun, sestina, villanelle. But it is his jabs which will kill you: "ten old men sit side-by-side comparing death" and alas "it is all management and math." Christiansen conjures "so many sharp encounters" and he knows how to "slice or chop in a single motion" to leave only the bones on your plate and all of these living ghosts in your head."

-Scott Ferry, author of *Sapphires on the Graves*

At heart in Rick Christiansen's *Not A Hero* is child-like curiosity paired with humility. I kept thinking as I read page to page of Wordsworth's line "the child is father of the man" from his poem "My Heart Leaps Up", how the wide-eyed innocence is in every page but at the same time there's loss and bittersweet forgiveness. From the difficult tenderness of "Ladybug" to the loving patience of "Postcards" to the frightened innocence of "Coffee Faith," Christiansen embodies the soul of a man learning, loving and letting go.

-Jonie McIntire, Poet Laureate of Lucas County, Ohio

"*Not a Hero*, Rick Christiansen's second poetry collection, epitomizes his simple, direct, evocative storytelling skills—prose poems without the telltale prose formatting. NOT A HERO is a story of life—a journey through Rick's eyes as he weaves tales of the lives of family, perhaps close friends, perhaps people he has observed. It's an engaging read, daubed, expertly, with wit, reflection, poignancy, at times humor, and unexpected phrases ("furniture as prophecy", "early bird catches the tumor"). Some of the poems will make you laugh (*We would accept you if we could…but we can't…so we won't.*); some will touch you profoundly ("Parakeet Tricks"). PS: If you're a reader of poem titles like me, you'll appreciate the clear, at times intriguing titles Rick has chosen for the vignettes in this collection such as "Borrowed Blood," "Why Men Should Not Own Parrots," "A Tapestry of Buzzing," "Coffee Faith," "The Honesty of Women"). Take a walk with Rick Christiansen through the door he opens in *Not a Hero.*"

-Lynda V. E. Crawford, author of *Washing Water*

"All the art that covered the previous century and the alleged "end of history" neglected to think that history could end over and over, and here are many of us poets wondering what we do in this new century we won't see the end of. In *Not a Hero*, Rick C. Christiansen gets his Whitman on and sings a song of himself, his heroes, and others he's met along the way. An eclectic mix for the most eclectic of times with pauses to refresh we will likely need to cherish as days go by."

-Chad Parenteau, Associate Editor *Oddball Magazine*, Stone Soup Poetry Author of *Can't Republic: Erasures and Blackouts*

Not a Hero

Poems by Rick Christiansen

Spartan
Press

Spartan Press
Kansas City, Missouri
spartanpresskc.com

Spartan
Press

Acknowledgments:

The author would like thank the editors of the following
publications where some of these poems first appeared
(in some form or another):

"Not a Hero:" *Rye Whiskey Review,*
"Killing Bob Dylan:" *Alien Buddha Press Pop Anthology,*
"Borrowed Blood:" *As It Ought To Be Magazine,*
"Why Men Should Not Own Parrots," "Fresh Eel," "Love
    Letter to a Poet:" *Oddball Magazine,*
"Clear Margins:" *Trailer Park Quarterly,*
"The Gods are too Loud," "Wink Back:" *Stone Poetry Quarterly,*
"We would Accept if we Could:" *Under the Bleachers Magazine*

Table of Contents:

For Kimberly Ross to whom I dedicate all of myself.

"There is a crack in everything, that's how the light gets in."

– Leonard Cohen, Anthem

Not a Hero

Just not yet shattered
Reflecting and bending light
We are all new glass

My father was past 80 when he finally began to tell us
    about the war.
It was his first war, when he was only 20.
He served during three conflicts.
But it was that first war that marked him.

It started when we found the box of his medals and
we told him that he was a hero.
He became angry. He rejected the label with scorn.
He told us…

That he knew heroic men.
But that he was not one of them.
He said…

First you get scared and you stay scared.
You are frightened for so long and so relentlessly.

That you get angry and you stay angry.
You are angry for so long and so relentlessly.

That you get stupid.
You start to take risks.
You do crazy things that you would never have imagined.

And if those crazy things don't get you killed,
well then, they give you medals.
But it was all just because you were afraid.
And you didn't want to be there.
You could not believe that you WERE there.
How the hell did it happen?

You were pissed at yourself, and the enemy, and
	your mission,
and the cold, and the dirt and the bullets, and the
	goddam army!

He said the good war movies got a lot of it right.
At least the newer ones.
But he said they couldn't get at his deepest memory of it all.

The smell.

He told us of the smell of his own skin
and of the men around him in the foxholes.

Once they had a break.
The Major told them to put the torn and worn uniforms
	that they had been
wearing for months into a pile.
A gigantic pile of filthy fabric.
And they doused it with kerosene to burn the stench and
	the lice.
And they all got cold showers.
And fresh uniforms were on the way.

But the new uniforms never got there.

Each man had to pick through the pile of kerosene soaked
     garments.
Trying to find something close to the right size.
With correct rank and insignia.

He said he spent two more months in another man's
     clothes.
And that it took a week before the stink was his own
     again,
even through the stench of kerosene.
But they were grateful.
At least the fuel killed the lice.

He said the cold that winter was worse than the artillery.
The shells came in waves.
There were lulls and valleys in the action.
But the cold was constant.

He said you got worried if it stopped hurting.
That meant the cold was winning.
So you would shake and stomp to bring back the pain
that told you that you were still alive.

And then he showed us his three belly buttons from the
     bullet wounds.
But this time he wasn't being silly like every time before.
This time he was in earnest.
For the first time he was bearing witness.
It wasn't a punchline anymore.

He told us all of these things almost quietly.

Quickly, and with an embarrassment bordering on
    shame.
But also some stubborn pride.

He just wanted us to know.

That he was not a hero.
You see.

Killing Bob Dylan

Men try to kill a thing before it can tell them the truth.
Bob was having none of that.
He hit Highway 61 hard.

Everything about him was elusive except for the words
and, of course, the music.
And, they almost got him on his Triumph Tiger.

But he was made of boot leather,
and non-filter cigarettes at 3:00 AM,
and promises that no man should have to keep.

So he licked his wounds
and was back on the road in a year.
Because he knew that it is magnificent to love something
that is broken.

And he loves us all like a Jewish Mother.
Doling out wisdom and criticism
wrapped in newspaper, and truth, and some hope.

He just wrote about what he read in the papers.
And when he saw a thing
he just said it.

Sure…he went electric.
But everybody was going deaf anyway
and he needed the volume.

And he went Country.
Cuz they would never look for him in Nashville
with a loaded gun.

To confect a life is hard,
abandoning the shackles of structure
without surrendering to chaos.

Ask any warrior.
Chaos/ breeds healing/ born from resolve.
And resolve is a paper sword.

Bob's resolve was born from a dog's belly
Ready to be expelled
in a nauseous heave.

Bob knew that the first sign of anything
can be a stop sign
or a crucifix.

He burned down the fetid house
without providing plans
to build another.

And he stole wisdom
from the abyss of
an asphalt parking lot.

Bob saw that we have an awful lot of meat in the
    refrigerator.
And he knew it would stain the furniture.
And he knew that we needed a container.

Bob saw that context has always been more important
    than punctuation.
That life should be a poem and not a memo.
Cuz the form forces you into discretion.

There is a sweetness to experiencing the end of things.
And men must surprise, even themselves, with their
    secrets.
Trying to build a fire that will survive the rain.

Bob knows—
a good person will only screw you if he has to…

Annie 2022

The whimper is like releasing steam
from a boiler. Incremental pressure
dropping, joints relax as they flex.

Pain too big to feel all at once,
needs too large to capture
in the boundaries of a moment:

desire an irritation—an itch.
She spasmodically plucks at the loose
skin on the back of her hand.

Feels the weight of the blankets,
toes tented at the foot of the bed.
He watches her stare at the button

on the morphine pump.
Sees her calculating her equation,
trying to reconcile relief with lucidity.

California Sketches 4x4

Anaheim 1955

The structures rise up out of the plundered orange
　　groves.
An edifice of imagination tempered by hope and greed.
Already lesser persons take a stand.
Filling the easement with fading opportunities.

Santa Monica 1967

The sand is firmly packed by drug addled heels.
Pounding like the surf to a Motown beat.
God has a work order in place.
The craftsmen are eager to begin.

East LA 1979

The donut shop sells malt liquor now.
A small Vietnamese woman gives change scornfully.
Dropped candy melts in pools by the curb.
It hasn't rained in a long time.

LA Streets 1991

High speed intoxication spawns police retaliation.
Rodney King is beaten beyond recognition.
89 seconds captured which makes the news.
Justice twinkles briefly, but then is lost.

The Weight of Bridges

Our struggle is a struggle to redeem the soul of America. It's not a struggle that lasts for a few days, a few weeks, a few months, or a few years. It is the struggle of a lifetime, more than one lifetime.

-John Lewis

I am SO very angry.
I feel betrayed by my culture.
I want to turn my back.
Hide behind my walls, waiting for Amazon deliveries
and the collapse of our republic.

"If you don't like it here...LEAVE!"
I will not leave.
John Lewis knew the shape of struggle,
it's sharp edges, it's relentless weight.
He was there when history pressed its hand to the earth
and left a scar.

On bridges, in courtrooms, in streets
where justice was just a whispered hope,
He laid himself down as a path.
He faced the tear gas, the batons, the hard edges of power,
with nothing but conviction.

Good trouble, he whispered,
as if the phrase could unlock doors
that had been welded shut for centuries.
Find the kind of trouble that cracks the veneer of denial,
that pulls truth into the light, even when everyone wants
to look away.
Good trouble, he called it—

The kind that bends steel,
Shatters glass,
And leaves a mark
on those who refuse to yield.

Good trouble does not ask for permission,
does not wait for the tide to turn.
It steps forward,
Knowing that the way is made
only by those who refuse to stand still.

Good trouble he knew,
Is not the absence of peace,
but the fight for its truth—
a weight that only the resolute can carry.
A weight carried by those who refuse to stand down.

Good trouble—
The kind that cracks open the heart of a nation
and lets the light flood in.
I will not run and hide.
I will bear the weight of bridges.

Ladybug

"Ladybug, ladybug, fly away home.
Your house is on fire and your children are gone."
—English nursery rhyme

He didn't know what alcohol was,
except that it smelled sharp.

Like the smell when
they gave him shots at the doctor.

She mixed it with lemonade when she was alone,
on hot afternoons, with only him for company.

She called him her best buddy.
Hugged him close,
then pushed him away.

Blew cigarette smoke into his eyes
until they burned and he could not catch his breath.

When she wasn't sad or mad or drinking or crying,
they made jigsaw puzzles together.

She would remind him to find
all of the pieces with straight edges.

They would build the border,
fill it with all of the other pieces,
sorted by color and subject.

Part of a fence/
red like the bricks/
blue from the sky.

She was drinking this afternoon
and sent him outside with a grape popsicle.

She was tired of his questions.
Crying, because she had slapped him.

The sun was too warm on his face
as he sat in the dirt of the weed filled yard.

The popsicle was gone now.
He was getting thirsty.

A lady bug landed on the back
of his hand.

Sitting very still,
`hoping she would not fly away,
he wanted to be her friend.

If he became very small or
she became very large,
they would fly away together.

They would make a new home for just the two of them.
It wasn't sad there.
It was quiet and calm.

They could go over the high fence,
Away from this dry choked place.
He would not be lonely.

But now the ladybug seemed restless
and her wings fluttered.
He knew she was going to fly away.

He sat on the packed soil,
thirsty and afraid to go in.

His mother would yell.
Hold him down with her knees,
kneeling on his arms.

Tell him that it was all *because* of him.
That she *too* was lonely and trapped.

And, they were out of grape popsicles.

Borrowed Blood

Haibun

The artist wandered the Polish wilderness. His art was born from borrowed blood. He followed hunters, men who saw him as an oddity, a specter haunting their trails. In the crisp air of the Eastern Carpathians, he traced the paths of their kills, the blood of deer, boar, and sometimes wolves, guiding him to his canvases. Today, he trailed a pair of hunters, their rough laughter carried on the wind. He moved silently, eyes sharp, until he found the fresh blood trail of their latest quarry. He crouched beside it, dipping his brush into the crimson smears. His canvas, a piece of white linen stretched over a frame, leaned against a tree. With deliberate strokes, the artist painted the scene of the hunt—The blood added a raw, visceral quality to his work, a macabre beauty that ink or paint could never capture. His hands moved with an urgency, a reverence, as if each stroke was a prayer. The forest was his cathedral, and the blood, immortalized in shades of red and brown, was his faith. Completed—he leaves the canvas at the base of the of the tree. The hunters would find it come morning, as they always did, and wonder at the ghost who followed them. They never knew his name.

Murders of crows watch
Satisfied with the outcome

Why Men Should not Own Parrots

A big Amazon Grey, that's what I'm not going to have.
The blank, feral countenance almost too much to bear.
Like looking into a mirror.

They live a long time,
such a commitment.

My friend had one once.
It went on a rampage.
Repeatedly.
Like a confused, angry child
it turned everything over
and then did it again.
Finally, exhausted, it sat confused.
Wondering why so much effort led to so little effect.

The mood swings are the hardest part.
A man needs stability.
And they bite.

You must feed them
every day.

And they will send scattered
seed husks to the floor
that may cause you to slip and fall
if you are not careful.

They are always hungry.

I have read that you can leave on the television.
The noise and light provide some stimulation
while you are away.

When you do arrive home, they become excited
and they try to hide their emotions with
kung fu kicks from the perch.

Waiting for you to make the first move
toward reestablishing a relationship that has diminished
in your absence.
Even if only for the day.

They are related to the dinosaurs
and seem afraid of the same extinction.
That is why they cling to your shoulder
Waiting for you to whisper your secrets to them.

They like repetition.
It makes them feel secure.

You must know what they need without being told.
Or, they become waspish and aloof.
Or, sometimes solicitous,
like a child who smells the candy in your pockets.

It is exhausting to be the object of such anticipation
without direction.
No wonder you delay your arrival longer each day.

Perhaps a parakeet or cockatiel
light enough to perch on your finger
will suffice?

Certainly, one of those would be harder to notice
when you are tired and do not wish to attend?

Where there is less weight, there is less gravity.
And the tantrums are smaller.

As the Crow Flies

You were in my dream last night.
We were in a balloon...not hot air...conventional helium
    or hydrogen
 I guess....
we had tanks and ballast.
You were the navigator
and you wanted us to go straight over the mountains
instead of zigzagging around them.
I was dubious...but we followed your plan and arrived
    safely.
Interestingly…
I have no idea where it was that we arrived to…
just that it was beyond the mountains
and that we had made very good time.

Apology to my ~~Ex-Girlfriends~~
Dead Houseplants

I was not able to keep
any of you alive. Never
planted deep. Not
enough sunlight or water.

No opportunity to properly
root, pessimistic at the first
sign of leaves browning
or stems drooping.

Soon uprooted completely,
every time
replaced with
fresh greenery.

I really
did want you
to flourish: but
there was this tree.

Planted seedling grew
for many years, I tended—
tall enough for shade
and sheltering children.

Then—rotting limbs.
The children left.
I was left,
sawing branches,

Even though I knew you
needed a gardener,
a partner to share
the sunlight.

Triple Word Score

I dream that we are playing Scrabble on the phone.
Word games from a distance.

Arguing over the EXACT placement of each tile.
It is so important to us both
that no cheating occur.

I imagine your look of concentration as you search
    through
your alphabet for the right combination of letters to
    unlock
the secret of the board.

Winning is not your goal.
You just want to make a good impression.

Epiphany

Immediate gestalt,
pieces paired.

Bond without friction.
Knowing without knowledge.

Together hum.
Soundless buzz.

Potential communicated
between laced fingers.

Entwine like threads
gathered and kept.

Intuitively saved—
for just this moment.

Once may have built pyramids together.
Now create structure—from this recognition.

Blocks stacked
on foundation discovered extant.

Your taste on my tongue.
Pulling your scent into myself.

Paradigm Shift

I hold within me an image of you
that is both crystalline and dynamic.
You are more than a fragment of my being.
I sense your dwelling and stirring within me.

You stretch out in the room I have built for you and
I feel the rhythm of your breath.

A void is filled where no void was known to be.
You are my choice without conscious decision.

I trace your intricacy with my mind.
I trace your form with my fingers.

You are known to me.

Fresh Eel

You are fresh eel
Cut into luxurious silken strips
I am sticky rice
Resting in small clumps

Both on the plate
Still separate
An expanse of porcelain
Between us

There is time for this

In the quiet of a long afternoon,
where shadows stretch like old memories,
two hands, weathered by time,
reach across the worn wood of a café table.

Her laugh is soft, like the sound of leaves
swirling in an Autumn wind,
his smile a slow sunrise,
warming skin long untouched by morning's light.

They speak of gardens,
of books read and forgotten,
of children grown and scattered
like seeds on the wind.
They smile at each other's memories.
Now better, shared.

In each pause, the weight of years—
not burdensome, but steady,
a rhythm they both know.

They do not rush,
for time, once an enemy,
now moves gently between them,
a patient observer.
There is time for this.

In the spaces between words,
they find a tenderness

that does not question,
a love that has shed the urgency of youth.

Together, they walk into the evening,
the sky an open canvas of gold and ash,
their steps measured,
their hearts quiet but full.

Couch Therapy

I see them wandering purposefully through the aisles of
   IKEA.
Masked, but eyes expressive of hope and a bit of searching
   desperation.

A scouting expedition from what was once called home.
What has now become womb, for more than a year.

Eyeing the fabrics hungrily. Eyes darting back and forth
from swatch to futon to comfy chair.

Furniture as Prozac.

Trying to turn what is beginning to feel like a prison
back into a nest.

You can tell how they have handled the year
by the way they engage with each possible purchase.

A thoughtful caress of a chair arm.
A full fledged drop into a deep leather sofa.

Wanting to commit to something.
Wanting to shift from a learned response of avoidance.

A flinch that has bled into even their dreams.

Afraid to choose something that looks delicate.
It is a time to be sturdy and firm for the long haul.

Afraid to choose too boldly.
It is best not to draw much attention just now.

You can see that they want to select for the future.
Furniture as prophecy.

And pillows, but just the right pillow.
On just the right chair.
In just the right corner.

Chosen with the certainty that its placement
will nudge things forward to a better day.

Wash Rinse Repeat

After Marilyn Chin's Altar (#3) from Broken Chord Sequence

Why cry over lost children?
They're meant to be gone.
Why cry over that reality?
We choose this ourselves.

Why cry over more bullets each day?
Why cry over the tiny coffins?
Why cry over tears of a mother?
Her wet face shines and reflects our sin.

Clear Margins

The waitress is a ginger, maybe 20, skinny and cheerful.
She brings more coffee and coconut pie.

Watch him devour a mouthful while he watches
a couple quietly bickering at another table.

He doesn't think they can tell he is watching them
if he uses the mirrors between the windows.

Focus on the arguing couple's toddler
who is running back and forth through the
warm sunny spot on the carpet created by the light
coming through the window of the diner.

He takes another bite of pie.

*If I have clear margins on this MRI scan, that means I
wait a year for another scan...*

More coffee.

Observe how the waitress favors the home health care
     nurse
who taught him wound care after the surgery. They both
     have nice hands.

Notice the sunlight shifting across the floor as he slowly
     eats his pie.

The toddler gets closer to his booth while chasing the warmth.

The old farmer comes in and sits at his usual place at the counter.

The waitress tells the farmer that he was on the edge of late for the lunch specials.

Man, I don't know if I can wait a year. Next Thursday is as far as I can see.

He thinks that he never wants to be late for anything again. Early bird catches the tumor.

That's funny.
He can wait a year.

Parakeet Tricks

She knew how to train parakeets to do tricks.
She was good at it as a girl.
She even got on local tv —in the early 1950s.
She showed her birds
pushing around ping pong balls and navigating
hoops and ramps that she had built herself.

She was a resourceful girl.

She was rewarded for the bird's compliance
with applause
that she never forgot.

When opportunity and instinct first collide
inspiration hears the crash
and rushes to the scene.

It took him more than a moment
to realize that the techniques she used
to make those birds bob and weave
—were the same
she used on his brother and himself.

Like a parakeet pushing ping pong balls up a ramp
it was his job to push his little brother
from place to place.

To keep him contained.
To never turn the wagon over or let him bump his head.

If there was a bruise
she must recognize the shape
of her own fist.
Or there was hell to pay.

No rough housing in the backseat.
Distractions can be dangerous.
—Anyway

When a two-door Mustang
is careening across the desert
at 100 mph.

So they counted dead jackrabbits
on the road to see...
who could get to 100 first.

And he always let his brother win.

Then they both got a tropical fruit Life Saver candy
instead of a slap.

She had exceptional instincts—
Although she had no formal training,
she knew how to find the strings.

And when to pull
And when to pluck
And you never even knew you were dancing.

Coffee Faith

Sestina

> *"The Child's faith is new ~*
> *Whole ~ like His Principle"*
>
> -Emily Dickinson

He contemplates the canisters from his chair,
sitting, staring from the kitchen table.
They are avocado green and lined up by size.
All sitting in a row on the wide counter.
Each is labeled. Each has its own name.
He focuses on the one named *Coffee.*

He has smelled but never tasted coffee.
The adults drink it eagerly, observed from his chair.
There is power in the things the grown ups name.
Job, car, money, coffee— faith in words at the table.
When the grown ups are asleep, he climbs on the
      counters.
He is four, but agile for his age and size.

Grown ups pay heed only to the things their size.
Small beyond notice, he thinks about the coffee.
To open that canister in curiosity— to have that
      encounter.
To get up there, all he need do is move his chair.
He slides the chair over from the table.
He is smart. He has taught himself to read the names.

There is magic in words. There is power in names.
He knows they ignore him because of his size.

They forget he is there when he sits at the table.
He watches them grow powerful as they drink the coffee.
He listens. Learns the names of things from his chair.
Today he is going to eat the coffee grounds on the counter.

He pushes the chair until it is pressed tight to the counter,
determined to swallow the power that comes with that name.
Rising onto his toes, he balances on the chair.
Stretching with his arms, he strains with deep sighs,
reaching until he grasps the canister named *Coffee*.
Climbing down carefully, he carries it to the table.

The bitter grounds burn his tongue, he trembles at the table,
wishing he could avoid this encounter.
Wanting the magic in this thing... he has faith in the coffee.

Lemon Grove

Villanelle

Lifted by safe arms into the sunlight.
Small child raised high toward the bright sky.
Teaching what is ripe, showing what is right.

Old man eager to share life with this sprite.
Wants to give the boy all he was denied.
Lifting with safe arms toward the sunlight.

Immigrant dreams manifest, hopes excite
an old man's telling before he will die.
Teaching what is ripe, knowing what is right.

Nurturing this boy, seeing without sight
the gaps in his young soul and healing by
lifting him safe up toward the sunlight.

The boy listens to learn, hanging on tight.
Blind grandfather points toward branches high.
Teaching what is ripe, showing without light.

And you, old man, now long gone from this fight.
Gift of your vision now seen in my eyes.
Lifted by safe arms into the sunlight.
Taught all that is ripe, knowing what is right.

Karma Thief

Haibun

When I was young...
I was in many ways, a thief, a liar, and a cheat...
But I have been thinking about it...
I went out of my way to only screw over assholes...
Somehow, I feel like that has impact on the karma...
Like when I was 10 and living in North Hollywood, there
    was this old lady who lived in another apartment
    next to us.
I think she had a pension and maybe a little bit of money
    and she was going blind...
And I ingratiated myself with her and she would give me
    a quarter to thread needles for her and stuff like that...
And I could've easily stolen from her or talked her out of
    all kinds of things, but I didn't because she was a
    good person...
On the other hand, the guy who ran the Los Angeles Times
    paper route I had was an asshole...
So I took off with three months worth of newspaper
    receipt money that I had collected, but never turned in.

The bird inhales
Tasting the intent of her prey

a boa constrictor to a mouse

In the grass, I slither near.
Little mouse, have you a fear?

Don't squirm, don't fret, just come on down.
In my belly, you'll soon be found.

So little mouse, it's time to part.
You'll be a snack, a work of art.

Fill up my belly, I have an urge.
You are quite small and not a splurge.

Your scampering days are now defunct.
Get ready mouse, you have been punked.

Zen Christmas Carol

Merry merry...
happy happy...
the tree hums.

It waits sturdy in the frozen howl.
Branches gesticulating upward
in a joyous dance of acceptance.

Little Red Wagon

It felt less like a dream and more like a memory.
I often did take our soiled clothes to the neighborhood
    laundromat.
I was 12, it was one of my jobs.
My little brother usually tagged along.

I was pulling our little red wagon.
It held a bulging denim duffle bag filled with our week's
    laundry.
My pockets were heavy with spare change
They bulged like the blue denim duffle.
They banged noisily against my thighs as we walked up
    the hill.
I pulled the wagon along.
I encouraged my brother to keep up.
I discouraged him from climbing into the wagon for a
    ride.
I imagined stuffing extra clothing into each washer.
Topping off each load, in hope of having surplus
    change, for candy after, for us both.

My brother behaved well when he thought there would
    be candy.
But his legs were tired as the hill was crested.
He ached to join the laundry duffel for a ride.
He could not resist and hopped into the wagon atop the
    duffel as we started downhill.
He saw me lose my grip on the wagon handle.
He saw me stumble out of its path.

At first, his screams were excitement as he felt speed and
wind and acceleration.

But soon he was afraid and his screeches accelerated at pace
with the careening wagon.

I watch helplessly from my vantage at the top of the hill.

The wagon crashes into the curb.

The denim duffel tumbles from the wagon, splits and
vomits clothes.

I run down the hill. The change in my pockets banging
painfully against my thighs.

I am no longer thinking of candy.

I only hope my brother has not been split open like the
denim bag.

Will there be blood?

Postcards

We sit across from one another at the old linoleum table. It rocks slightly each time one of us rests a hand or forearm onto it. She places postcards on the table between us as I absently pick at the worn linoleum, creating small flakes which I then brush to the floor.

She arrays the faded rectangles across the center of the table like a film editor planning her story. I imagine a process occurring, image supporting idea, given form by words, informed by rhythm.

She almost whispers when she says, "I went to France the Summer I turned 17. I went alone, without friends or family. It is a long story."

She hesitates and seems to contemplate saying more. A shiver of sadness seems to scatter her face for a moment. Then she sighs with an expression of resolve.

"I made friends with these postcards that I found and purchased in shops and railroad kiosks. We spoke to each other. Each card told me a story. Each, revealed to me a piece of where it had been and I told each of them where I was going."

I sipped my tea and listened to our breathing as I watched her contemplate which card would be placed next from the pile in front of her, considering proximity of each to the other. Knowing a story changes depending on where you stand and with whom.

"This card was local to the village in which I stayed. It is a picture of the butcher shop. The butcher had only one hand. I would watch him make the steaks and chops. He would place the meat on the block carefully. Arranging it so as to make the intended entry point of the blade most accessible. He would then pick up the knife or cleaver and slice or chop in a single motion."

As she told me the story, she rearranged the postcards in front of her, mirroring the motions of the butcher as she was describing him, now only using the one hand, making a vertical chopping motion with the rectangle she was holding. Her other hand resting unheeded next to her cup of cooling Camomile tea.

"He would next lay down the implement and again arrange the meat for a cut."

She continued to make the chopping motion with her hand. Almost absently now, but with rising volume in her voice.

"Again and again he would repeat these movements until he had enough for the platter he placed each day in the window of the shop."

I sip my tea and sink into the rhythm of her story and the slight rocking of the table as we shift across from one another. She breathes deeply for several moments and then speaks again in almost a whisper.

"I think he lost the hand in the war. But, who knows. He was a butcher. So many sharp encounters."

She places the postcard of the shop gently down next to another faded card depicting a young girl looking at a park lake while trying to ignore the ducks at her feet.

"These postcards are still the best friends that I have made. We still talk to each other. The conversations help me to recapture my life from memory. And now they help me to talk to you."

I rise and kiss my Grandmother on her temple. I take a knife from the drawer and begin to prepare lunch.

The Honesty of Women

I like the honesty of women.
I have discovered that… as my male friends slowly die off.
I find myself with empty slots in my batting line up.
Nobody is left to play third base.

I need the play of conversation.
I need to defend my opinions.
I find my own boundaries by bumping into those of
    others.

Older men can shrink from intimacy.
Unless it has grown unheeded, like a weed
in the backyard of a long term acquaintance.
We surprise even ourselves with the disclosure of our
    secrets.
Blurted during the third beer and only after the new
    sports season
has been argued and put to bed.

The contents of our souls are guarded, locked away until
    years
of friendship have eroded the tumblers of the mechanism
    and a key fits in.

And these old dogs are dying.
And I am still here.
And I still crave that connection.
And I cannot wait years to build that shed of trust with
    other men.
So…I like the honesty of women.

No Delivery

The waitress looks like the one who served him in college
at a little KC pizza place built in the shell of a former
Dairy Queen.

It was run by three guys who said they were Bolivian,
and brothers.
The pizza was good and cheap.

But then they got busted for cocaine distribution.
That was the secret of their success.

It used to be you could tell a waitress that she reminds
you
of somebody and she might be flattered.

Now he does not dare.
Since the surgery, since they removed his eye.

The pizza place reopened. The pizza tasted cheap.
They didn't have that drug money to buy the good
cheese.

It is hard to do anything without the good cheese.
It is hard to do anything when they stare at where the
eye should be.

Like a car with one headlight.
He doesn't want to be a fucking pirate.

Aubade to my Oral B

As first light filters through the frosted glass,
I see your worn and frizzled bristles.
You stand so tall and proud.

Star of my morning regimen.
Always ready for a dab of paste,
a brisk morning stroll across my molars.

But now, bent and aged,
I fear the time has come
for our farewell.

I hold you—firm and close.
My glance into the mirror affords
a snapshot of us two—an image to remember.

I retain my grasp on you,
reflected in the dawn glow.
One last time together.

Our dental dance informed by
the melody of water splashing
into the sink beneath us.

Companion to my gums.
Noble plaque catcher.
Friend to incisors.

Your tousled head rinsed clean.
I contemplate this parting thus:
reflecting on your faded handle.

Your sister waits in the cabinet drawer.
Her time now come as morning passes.
One last shake for you—a parting sigh.

Toxic Teaching

Sestina

All content compiled and excerpted from e-mail
   correspondence with Timberland High School concerning
   my grandson over a 30 day period.

School District Families
We wanted to make you aware that yesterday
the Environmental Protection Agency (EPA) notified us
about possible mercury exposures. Thanks for checking in.
He tends to spend a lot of time on his phone. That is how
   he's studying at home.
Focused effort is critical. I know he can remember.

We are all trying to keep students in the building. We must
   remember.
A limited number of other District Families
may have been exposed to mercury at home.
Other District personnel, gave each building the "all-clear"
   yesterday,
contacted us and were checking in
on the health and safety of our students, which is so
   important to us.

We've worked closely with the EPA, they notified us.
Ask questions about the quizzes, I know, we know... he can
   remember.
Ask me to go over his flash cards or quizlets while
   checking in.
Rule out any mercury being brought into our buildings
   by other District Families.

The Environmental Protection Agency (EPA) gave each
building the "all-clear" yesterday.
You must let us know if he was exposed to mercury at
home.

Exposures did not occur at school. He will be working
from home.
Although these in-class reviews would not be a miracle
cure, they are important to us.
Tylor had not communicated with me yesterday.
He is welcome to come in. I know he can remember.
Ask me to check over his flash cards like other District
Families.
Reviews would not be a miracle cure. But, thanks for
checking in!

Who may have been exposed to mercury? The student is
welcome to come in
before or after school, and he will also be working from
home.
We are concerned about the possible mercury exposures
in District Families.
So out of an abundance of caution, it definitely wouldn't
hurt to notify us.
It is important. He can remember.
Thank you for your open and honest conversation
yesterday.

Mercury being brought into our buildings yesterday
through shoes, clothes, etc. So many parts are missing.
Please come in.
He tends to spend a lot of time on his phone. We must
remember.

Other District students are working from home.
They are also important to us.
We thank you for your conversation. We are families.

We've worked closely with the EPA since yesterday.
Health and safety of our students is important to us.
Make the best use of his class time. Check over his flash
  cards. I know he can remember.

Kaddish

Ghazal

The ten old men sit side-by-side comparing death.
Say, we grow warm—the planet now is sharing death.

Say, with each new storm and flood the wounds grow
    deeper.
While neighbors turn their heads away—just daring
    death.

No masks—no shots—the death toll just keeps rising, so
these men know, there's no point to try despairing death.

They make their peace in any soil that they find.
And know there is no stake in us foreswearing death.

The ten old men (begin to chant) their Kaddish now.
Lament to face a stern and quite uncaring death.

They sing to all the things that we are losing now.
A song of faith that brings us to unerring death.

The old men call to bees— and to the buffalo.
They chant (for all the things) that will be wearing death.

The content of old men's hearts—inform their prayers.
They try to guard themselves from *known* impending
    death.

They wish for all, and pray for each, escape from death.
Pray—(add *my* name) to chanting for lamenting death.

The Gods are too Loud

"In his hands Hercules took his shield, all glittering: In the center and upon the shield Proioxis (Pursuit) and Homados (Tumult) were wrought."

—Hesiod "The Shield of Hercules"

The Gods are too loud
and I cannot hear them

They wail from my pipes
and screech from my ductwork

I am trapped by the sound
into deafness. Left

to worship Homados
Noise speaks danger

Crouching beneath
whistling metal

Bursting silence

Rusty Palace

Under the metal canopy's shade,
A carport stands stoic and unadorned,
Like a weary traveler seeking respite,
From the relentless sun and rain.

Its steel beams hum with stories untold,
Of rusted dreams and forgotten journeys,
Where old cars rest like tired souls,
Nursing wounds of neglect and theft.

No polished facade or false charm here,
Just raw utility and weathered grace,
A sanctuary for the worn-out and weather-beaten,
In a world that rarely slows down.

In the shadow of this unassuming shelter,
Life pauses briefly, a cigarette in hand,
As the day fades into a haze of asphalt and hope,
Beneath the indifferent gaze of the moon.

Road Salt Pantoum

A body like an old Chevy, corroded and worn,
reckless driving, and salt that won't wash away.
It is all management and math, resolve reborn—
Promise yourself, "I won't," and face each day.

Reckless driving, and salt that won't wash away,
Tap into a reserve tank, untouched through your prime.
Promise yourself, "I won't," and face each day,
Never back down, hold steady through time.

Tap into a reserve tank, untouched through your prime.
Never give up; will found anew.
Never back down, hold steady through time,
A body survives when resolve pulls it through.

A body survives when resolve pulls it through.
Cold winds bite, and the roads freeze again.
A steel frame bends but always holds true,
Fighting the seasons, through loss and gain.

Cold winds bite, and the roads freeze again.
Rust creeps in, unyielding, unkind.
Fighting the seasons, through new loss and pain,
Drive onward, even when the map's hard to find.

Rust creeps in, unyielding, unkind.
Each mile a battle, each turn a test.
Drive onward, although the map's hard to find,
Pushing forward, refusing to rest.

Never give up; will found anew.
Your body, an old Chevy, corroded and worn.
It ONLY survives when resolve pulls it through.
It's all management; resolve reborn.

Poem About My Son

I have never written a poem about my son.

Perhaps it is because I came back to writing late.
After my relationship with him
had started an inexorable slide
toward him becoming MY patriarch.

I live under him now.
In his basement.
It is a nice walk out.

Perhaps I am still
wearing down the path
smoothing the trail
of our new dynamic.

He is becoming the arbiter of our future together.

I have to know what I am writing about— to write it.
This is a new country.
I must travel its roads first—before I speak.

In the special forces they have a saying:
Slow is smooth.....smooth is fast.
I once changed his diapers.
One day he will change mine—or pay someone.
We will use our history together to make this transition—
smooth.

I am digesting this new son who is now the household
    father.
It is a new economic model.
He is now, the means of production.
I have become his consumer.
I am his client.

I *will* write a poem about him.
Smooth—but not *too fast!*

Love letter to a Poet

I think my affections would still be intact if you were a
    Notary
Your elegance and stealth would be apparent even on
    embossed documents
But your clever and elegant hand that so effortlessly
    untangles misshapen metaphors
Would be less obvious on a contract or deed
The poem is the vehicle with which you carry me to these
    unanticipated landscapes and sometimes destinations
You always make me feel better
Except when you don't
You see that it is ok to color outside of the lines sometimes
But that it should always be on purpose
You do not seduce me
But I do seduce myself on your behalf
There is beautifully crafted work
That I can enjoy for its structure
And the clever way it intricately solves problems
With deft shifts of word and line
But it is sometimes sterile
Your poetry never is…
Your words grow from a very rich dark earth
More satisfying than simply grazing scholarship
You sing the savage greedy song
Of mine before yours
And I tilt my head to listen
To find balance and tempo
I come to be tickled by phrases
But am instead changed

And so it is that each new tapestry
Changes me to be ready for the next that will come
And so it is that I am new and renewed

Wink Back

There is a poem in the hallway half bathroom sink.
I hear stanzas when I wash my hands in there.
The cadence stops when I look into the mirror.

There is a poem in the bird feeder on my porch.
It drops rhymes onto the ground with the scattered seeds.
The birds peck at each word as if searching for new flavors.

There is a poem under my pillow.
I can feel the lump when sleep will not come.
In my dreams the words wind around my history and make
untangled knots.

There is a poem at the bottom of my bowl of soup.
It winks at me as I lift broth onto my spoon.
I wink back as I swallow.

We would accept you if we could...
but we can't...so we won't.

Poetry journal submission rejection letters – a comic sampling.

Dear Poet,

Thank you for letting us consider your work. Your poem has one line we found incredibly evocative and very intriguing. Unfortunately, the rest of your verse has the consistency of baby vomit. If you have any other work that is less like baby vomit, we welcome the chance to reject it also!

-Keep writing!

Dear Poet,

Thank you for allowing us to reject your work. We found reading your poem to be universally painful for our editorial staff. However, we enjoy punishing our team. Although this poem is "not for us", we welcome additional submissions in the future as we LIKE to watch our staff suffer. It gives us pleasure. So.... much....pleasure....

Are you suffering?

-Keep writing!

Dear Poet,

What are you wearing? Right now? Are you holding a pen....are you holding it "firmly"? You are a BAD poet! So....so...BAD! You need punishment.

Assume the position!

Oh....and we hated your poetry.

-Keep writing!

Dear Poet,

Thank you for allowing us to consider your multi-media project, "Sestinas for all Members". Although our editorial staff admires your ekphrastic project of writing sestinas to dick pics, we are currently only considering dick pic Haiku.

-Keep writing!

Dear Poet,

Our associate editor, Bob, read your recent submission and promptly ended his tenure with our publication in horror and disgust.

We hated Bob.

Thank you for your submission. Unfortunately it is not what we are looking for. But Bob was a DICK, so you have really helped us out here. Just sayin!

-Keep writing!

Dear Poet,

Thank you for your submission dated May 17, 1974. We have reviewed it carefully for a very long time. Unfortunately, we find your prose a bit old fashioned and perhaps more appropriate for a simpler time, pre-21st Century. We welcome your future submissions!

-Keep writing!

Dear Poet,

We really wanted to publish your work. We really... really..did want to do it. Our entire team here is in severe distress. We appreciate that your work comes from a "special" place inside of you. We are SO privileged to get to experience your poetry. Each member of our staff has been profoundly changed by your work.

Unfortunately, the team has very reluctantly chosen to go a different direction.

Please do not submit to us again for at least three years. Rejecting you again too soon would be too painful for us to bear.

-Keep writing!

Procrastination

Haibun

A squirrel scampered across the yard, and I was mesmerized. How effortlessly it avoided work, darting about with no deadlines. I found myself out on the porch, watching it, envying its freedom. Time slipped by unnoticed, the sun inching toward the horizon.

The clock ticks.

A blank page waits.
Squirrel laughs from the tree tops—

Rick Christiansen is a former corporate executive, stand-up comedian, actor and director. His work can be found in *MacQueen's Quinterly, Oddball Magazine, Stone Poetry Journal, The Rye Whiskey Review, As It Ought to Be Magazine, Trailer Park Quarterly North American Review* and other publications. His first full length poetry volume, *"BONE FRAGMENTS"*, was published last year by Spartan Press. He has been nominated for a Spirit Award and a Touchstone Award for his work. He is the co-host of SpoFest, an advisory member of The Writer's Place and a member of The St. Louis Writers Guild. He lives in Missouri with his wife Kim and dog "B."

This project was made possible, in part, by generous support from the Osage Arts Community.

Osage Arts Community provides temporary time, space and support for the creation of new artistic works in a retreat format, serving creative people of all kinds — visual artists, composers, poets, fiction and nonfiction writers. Located on a 152-acre farm in an isolated rural mountainside setting in Central Missouri and bordered by ¾ of a mile of the Gasconade River, OAC provides residencies to those working alone, as well as welcoming collaborative teams, offering living space and workspace in a country environment to emerging and mid-career artists. For more information, visit us at www.osageac.org

Osage Arts Community